CALIFORNIA
WINE COUNTRY

A PICTURE MEMORY

Text
Bill Harris

Captions
Ros Cocks

Design
Teddy Hartshorn

Photo Editor
Annette Lerner

Photography
Frank S. Balthis
Colour Library Books Ltd
FPG International
Robert Holmes
Michael Schaeffler

Commissioning Editor
Andrew Preston

Editorial
David Gibbon

Production
Ruth Arthur
Sally Connolly
Andrew Whitelaw

Director of Production
Gerald Hughes

CLB 2861
© 1992 Colour Library Books Ltd, Godalming, Surrey, England.
All rights reserved.
This 1992 edition published by Crescent Books,
distributed by Outlet Book Company, Inc., a Random House
Company, 40 Engelhard Avenue, Avenel, New Jersey 07001.
Printed and bound in Singapore.
ISBN 0-517-07273-4
8 7 6 5 4 3 2 1

CALIFORNIA
WINE COUNTRY
A PICTURE MEMORY

CRESCENT BOOKS
NEW YORK · AVENEL, NEW JERSEY

Back in the days when Julius Caesar was leading his legions through the land known as Gaul, the Romans took grape cuttings along to establish vineyards in their wake. The scheme wasn't so much an attempt to guarantee a free flow of wine in their new provinces, but to keep the locals under their thumb. A vineyard, like Rome itself, isn't built in a day, and the Romans knew that a community that spent a generation or more propagating grapes wasn't going to pack up and move before it could benefit from the fruits of its labors. More important, viticulture is the kind of hard work usually associated with coal mining, and the Romans also knew that people who labored in the vineyards from dawn to dusk would be too tired at the end of the day even to think of throwing off the conquerors' yoke.

The idea worked nearly everywhere they went, but nowhere quite as well as in Gaul, where the hillsides of Burgundy and the blessed soil of Bordeaux were soon producing the best wines in the Empire. Such serendipity should have been cause for celebration, but the Romans found it cause for alarm, and to eliminate the competition to vineyards closer to home, the Emperor decreed in 92 A.D. that all the vines in Gaul should be uprooted. Fortunately for the future of France, the order was ignored in many places, and two-hundred years later another Emperor, after having tasted some of the clandestine provincial product, countermanded it and the way was cleared for producing wines that are still the yardstick for judging all others.

Almost two-thousand years later, in the mid-1970s, the yardstick was applied in a blind tasting in Paris. An Englishman just back from a visit to California invited a group of prestigious experts – restaurateurs, writers and critics, and even government officials charged with maintaining the quality of French wines – to compare what he had found in the States to what they all considered the world's finest.

When their choices were identified for them, the French experts were mortified. They had picked not one, but two California wines as the best in the tasting. Not only that, but six of the top eleven had come from California's Napa Valley. There was nothing for it but to publish the results, and if faces were red in Paris they were wreathed in smiles in the Napa Valley. Californians had known for a long time that their wines were as good as any in the world, but from that moment on the world didn't have to take their word for it. Not only did some of the most respected experts say they were good, without the influence of any American salesmanship, mind you, but they agreed that they were possibly better. The world sat up and took notice.

The French argued that one tasting doesn't establish a trend any more than one robin heralds a spring, and they had a point. But the trend started anyway, probably because the wines the experts compared came from the same types of grapes, not always possible with wines from different countries. The reds were Cabernet Sauvignon, considered the superior reds of Bordeaux, and the whites were the product of the Pinot Chardonnay grape, the best Burgundy has to offer. The 1973 Cabernet

Sauvignon the experts chose came from the Stag's Leap Wine Cellars, not exactly a household name back then, especially compared to the competition which included the 1970 vintages of Château Mouton Rothschild and Château Haut-Brion. The 1973 vintage Chardonnay from California's Château Montelena was judged superior to a 1973 Bâtard-Montrachet, which most oenophiles agreed was among the finest France had to offer.

In many ways, the whole episode was a lot like comparing your kids to your sister's kids. The origins of the vines may be the same, but they are individuals and the resemblance to one another is probably irrelevant. It's significant that the Paris tasting didn't involve any Americans at all. California winemakers are well aware of the European traditions, but they don't usually invite comparisons because their wines are developed for the American taste in food, which, although it is European-based, too, is as unique as a bottle of California wine.

Comparing their wines is a lot like comparing California itself to Europe. They grow grapes in both places, but the similarities begin to dwindle once that fact has been established. The key to a fine wine is the right balance of sugar, which produces alcohol, and acidity, which gives the wine its aroma and taste. And the key to producing an exactly right balance is temperature. Too little heat retards the development of sugar and produces a weak wine; but too much of it bakes out the acidity, and the resulting wine will have little more character than a bottle of grape juice. In Europe, the climatic zones considered ideal for different varieties of grapes run from south to north, and the districts devoted to them have been established, often by law if not by climate, for centuries. In California it isn't quite that simple.

For almost the whole length of the state, the Coast Range extends inland for about forty miles and holds back the cold ocean air from the parallel valleys between its ridges. Thanks to the warm Japan current a few miles out, the California coast is almost always under a fog bank about 2,000 feet thick, and when the temperature goes up inland, the fog tends to move onshore. The mountains hold it back in most places, but in spots where there are gaps in the hills the fog rolls in under the rising warm air and cools some of the valleys as efficiently as a thermostatically-controlled air conditioning system. In general, those valleys and the hillsides around them are where the vineyards are, and microclimates within them allow varieties that are traditionally scattered hundreds of miles apart in Europe

to grow side by side in California.

But in the final analysis the comparison seems almost ludicrous, considering that vineyards have been flourishing in France, Germany and Italy for more than two millennia, and only as recently as two centuries ago the queen of California's wine country, the Napa Valley, was still waiting to be discovered. Indians had been there for thousands of years, as had the redwood forests above it, but until the 1820s the valley's main attraction was the hot springs at the base of Mt. St. Helena, which served as a sort of aboriginal health spa that brought red men from up and down the coast in search of relief from their aches and pains. White men in the form of Spanish missionaries had begun marching up the California coast in search of converts in 1769, but it took them another fifty years to get as far north as Sonoma. The Franciscans carried grape cuttings with them, but making wine was only a sideline at the twenty missions they established, until a trapper named George Yount arrived in the Napa Valley in 1831. The Mexican governor, General Mariano Vallejo, took a liking to him and rewarded him for his tips on civilizing the wilderness by giving him a land grant that included almost all of the valley. Yount settled down on his rancho and began raising mission grapes. His plan was to make wine for his own table, but it was soon apparent that the vines were as happy in their new home as Yount was, and his vineyards, tended by Indian laborers, became more important than his herds of sheep and cattle.

The forming of the California Republic, and the Gold Rush, brought new people into the Napa Valley, but not all of them were adventurers or fortune hunters. Word had reached Europe about Yount's vineyards, and German winemakers began arriving, too. The first of them was Charles Krug, who bought a ranch near St. Helena and built California's first commercial winery. Like Yount and the Franciscans, he grew mission grapes, but at almost the same time, across the ridge in the next valley, a Hungarian entrepreneur named Agostin Haraszthy imported cuttings from European vineyards and created the Buena Vista winery in the shadow of the Sonoma Mission. He was quickly followed by Jacob Schram and Jacob and Frederic Beringer, who introduced French growing and winemaking techniques to the Napa Valley, but also brought a German architectural style to their wineries. They brought their sense of business along with them, too, and by 1880 there were more than six hundred vineyards in the valley. There was no doubt in anybody's mind that the infant industry would eventually become as important to California as the gold in those hills to the east.

But fate had other things in store. Almost overnight, vigorously healthy vines began withering away, and when they were pulled up it was found that their root systems were almost completely destroyed. There was no villain to be seen, but experienced vineyardists knew it was a microscopic creature known as *phylloxera vastrix*, a louse that considers grape roots a delicacy. Ironically, *phylloxera* is a native American, but investigations hinted that it had reached California in the stock Haraszthy brought with him from Europe. But the investigators were less interested in finding the source than in coming up with a cure, and during the time it took to do so many of the Northern California vineyards vanished under a sea of grass.

Eventually they noticed that vines with native American rootstock were unaffected by the plague, and it became obvious that over time American vines had built up an immunity to the creature that caused it. The solution was to graft Old World grapes to New World roots, but it took ten more years of hard work to make the vineyards productive again.

Then, about twenty years after that, disaster struck again. In 1919, the required number of states ratified the Constitution's Eighteenth Amendment, and a year later it became a federal offense to manufacture or sell intoxicating liquors. Although the dictionary characterizes liquor as the product of distillation, the legal definition extended to fermented products like beer and wine, and no amount of arguing could change it. Some California vintners secured special licenses to produce sacramental and medicinal wines, some others winked at the law and went right on pressing their grapes. But in the main, most complied by turning their vineyards into orchards to give them a cash crop of walnuts and prunes. In the process equipment in the wineries began falling apart from lack of use and maintenance and, even worse, skilled vintners had to search for new careers and experienced vineyard workers were forced to move away.

When the drought finally ended in 1933, the California wine industry was a shambles, but there was a market out there. After fourteen years of drinking nothing at all or making do with the junk bootleggers provided, America was thirsty. California responded by shipping the product of tough-skinned grapes with a minimum of aging, and the better it sold the more they shipped. Americans drank it, but there wasn't much about it to enjoy, and once the novelty wore off, the consensus was that there wasn't much to be said about California wine except that it had a nice kick and there was plenty of it. It wasn't what serious vintners had in mind.

Fortunately, their minds weren't closed and they were willing to listen to the experts at the University of California, which had begun researching the science of oenology as far back as the 1870s. The academics suggested that rather than letting nature take her course, the winemakers should give her a boost with a little technology. Tradition stayed in the oak barrels used for aging, but when the scientists were able to prove that, during fermentation, glass-lined, stainless steel tanks with modern temperature controls made a more flavorful wine than the oak tanks that have served European wineries for hundreds of years, metal tanks began to dot the landscape. The scientists also suggested that grapes would ripen better if the vines were trained to reach for the sun, and the Californians moved another few centuries ahead in their game of catch-up with the longer-established Europeans. The university also grants degrees in the science, and its graduates have replaced many of the Old-World craftsmen Prohibition had driven away. But tradition and pride are still the most important qualities in the people who make wine, and are as highly regarded in California as a string of degrees.

No one needs a college education or even an educated palate to know that vines transplanted from Europe to America produce a different kind of grape, but from the beginning the people responsible for marketing wine felt safer giving them European names. If a wine was made from red grapes, it was called "Burgundy," and any white wine was called "Chablis." There still isn't any regulation about the generic wines shipped from California vineyards beyond the laws regarding alcohol content, which allows for ten to fourteen percent. They can be made from any grape variety, as long as the end product has the right color and the taste is in the right ballpark. But for all vagueness of the rules and regulations, the quality of what Americans frequently call "jug wine" usually amazes Europeans who grew up drinking "vin ordinaire."

The rules about varietal wines are more specific. The names can only be used if the wine gets such characteristics as taste and aroma from at least fifty-one percent of a specific grape variety. The percentage is higher in Europe, but geography limits the availability of particular varieties from district to district. Grapes considered suited only to Germany thrive in California, and so do the noble French varieties. The law also mandates that seventy-five percent of the grapes used for any vintage-dated wine must be from the same county, but there is no rule that forces a vintner to ferment it there. On the other hand, the practice of dating wines is often considered little more than an unnecessary tradition to California vintners. Because of its unique climate, there is almost never a year when the grapes don't ripen properly; never anything but a vintage year, as far as most Californians are concerned. Even the law thumbs its nose at the idea by allowing as much as five percent of any bottle to come from a different year than the one on the label. But the dates are useful to anyone looking for an encore of a pleasurable experience, and if every year is a vintage year, some are naturally better than others. In general, the main appellation is simply, "California," but individual regions such as the San Joaquin Valley and the Coast Counties also have their own. But none of them, quite unlike the system used in Europe, has much to do with climate.

Even the time-honored laws of other countries have little impact on the Californians. The French are quite tough with their rules regarding any sparkling wine made anywhere except in their own Champagne region. They even took Italian, Spanish and German vintners to court and won the right to keep the name in France. But they didn't bother in the case of the Californians, who had been producing champagne since the 1880s and made no bones about calling it what it was. But, ironically, when the French themselves invaded California and began producing champagne on the other side of the Atlantic, they discreetly called it "Napa Valley Brut." And it wasn't as though they didn't have a valuable marketing tool that could have made their product an even better seller. The winery that produces it, Domaine-Chandon at Yountville, is owned by Moët, the largest producer of champagne in France.

Quite simply, the California wine business is a free-for-all, but the end result of what probably seems like anarchy in the Old Country is some very good wine.

The hidden reason is the market. As a race, Americans have never been teetotallers, but since the first immigrants began arriving in the fifteenth century one of their main goals in life was to put aside the traditions they left behind in Europe. Chief among them was drinking wine. As the great waves of newcomers began arriving from the Mediterranean countries a century or two later, the enjoyment of wine was one of the pleasures they refused to give up, and their new neighbors, who resented them anyway, fixed on wine-drinking as a symbol of the lower classes. The situation continued for several generations before the prejudices were finally broken down, but it gave California marketers a tough hurdle to deal with. Even today, America ranks thirtieth among the nations of the world in per-capita wine consumption. It might rank even lower were it not for Ernest and Julio Gallo, the children of immigrants themselves, who went into the business with no previous experience beyond what they learned about winemaking from the Public Library in Modesto. But, at the same time, they had a rare understanding of the American market. They began with dessert wines and then pushed ahead with a potent, lemon-flavored port-based concoction they called Thunderbird. When it had run its course, the scientists they had added to their staff came up with Pink Chablis, a sugar and carbon-dioxide-laced mixture of rosé and white grapes. And so it went. The combination of tailor-made products and aggressive marketing made the Gallos a name to be reckoned with in the wine business. Eventually theirs was the biggest winery in the world, with huge tank farms dominating the Modesto landscape and a bottle factory that spews out jugs twenty-four hours a day.

But although marketing is as critical to the wine business as the California sunshine, and many wineries are the property of multinational corporations, there are still hundreds of vineyards and wineries run as family operations. And many of them don't produce enough wine to ship out of the state. But from a visitor's point of view, it adds the joy of discovery to the pleasures of the countryside.

Facing page: rolling vineyards of the Glen Ellen Winery, lying above the Valley of the Moon in California's second wine-producing area, Sonoma County. This is one of the region's oldest estates and was built in the 1860s. It has been restored and modernized over the past decade.

Top left: Clear Lake, in Lake County, on California's North Coast. Wild flowers bring cheer to a bare spring vineyard (center left) in Mendocino County, California's northernmost wine-producing area. Fetzer Winery in Hopland (below), is the largest in Mendocino County. This building used to be the High School. This winter scene is in the Russian River area (bottom left), Sonoma County. The rainy season lasts December through February, after which these bare skeletal vines will begin to sprout the new season's leaves. The patchwork of vines in Sonoma County (overleaf), second only to Napa Valley for its wine production, covers in excess of 30,000 acres and serves over 100 wineries.

Alexander Valley, in the Sonoma County Russian River region, boasts many quality wineries. Jordan Winery is particularly imposing, with a sumptuous dining room (facing page top), and sweeping drive (facing page bottom). Simi Winery (below), though thriving now, has had a checkered past in which it has changed hands many times. The winery is owned at present by the French wine producers Moët Hennessy. Overleaf: mist lies low over Boonville, west of the Russian River region.

Visitors to Sonoma County might wish to pause between wine tastings to take a tour of the House of Happy Walls (these pages), situated northeast of Glen Ellen in Jack London State Park. The house was built in 1922 by Charmian London, widow of the author Jack London, and is now a museum of the couple's possessions. The roll-top desk and dictaphone (below) were custom made. The tile-floored dining room (facing page bottom) was inspired by the Londons' visits to the South Seas.

Old hop barns (top left, center left, and bottom left), relics of Sonoma County's beer-brewing past, dot the countryside. Chateau Souverain (top left) is today a sizable winery which is open to visitors and has a pleasant restaurant. The Hop Kiln Winery (center left) is registered as a California Historical Landmark. The signpost (above) gives directions to a cluster of Sonoma County's most famous wineries. In the spring, mustard blooms beneath the still-bare vines (below and facing page top). Dry Creek Vineyard (facing page bottom) was founded in 1972 by its present owner David Stare. Overleaf: Cabernet Sauvignon grapes, pride of Sonoma County.

Some of Sonoma County's wineries date back to the nineteenth century. Buena Vista (top left), the oldest winery in the region, was founded in 1857 by Agoston Haraszthy, a Hungarian emigré. Glen Ellen Winery (center left) and the Grist Mill Inn Restaurant (bottom left) were built in the 1860s and 1838 respectively. Lyeth Winery (above), a small Swiss-run concern, produces only one red and one white wine. Sebastiani Winery (below), by contrast, produces a wide range of wines. Facing page: overshadowed by snow-peaked mountains, like Mt. St. Helena, the California vineyards have a beauty all their own. Overleaf: Souverain Winery, north of Healdsburg.

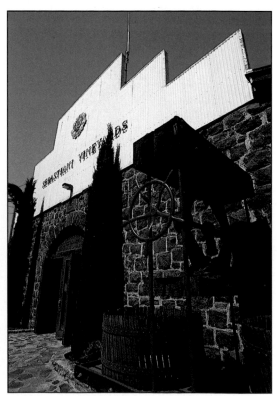

Calistoga (below), at the northernmost end of the Napa Valley Wine Way, is the center from which to visit the Chateau Montelena, Schramsberg, Stonegate, Sterling and Cuvaison vineyards. A resort of long-standing, the town is famous for its hot springs (top right and center right). If you are in this area it is worth visiting Old Faithful Geyser on Tubbs Lane which spouts sixty-foot showers of hot water and steam every forty minutes. The Calistoga Depot (bottom right) with its specialty shops is also worth a visit.

28

Built in 1969, Sterling Winery (top left, center left, and facing page top) has a stylized Grecian appearance and occupies a spectacular position on a hilltop overlooking the Napa Valley. Sculptures in the gardens of Clos Pegase Winery (bottom left) are part of proprietor Jan Shrem's philosophy of placing wine among the other art treasures of the world. Schramsberg (above) was rescued from ruin in 1964 by Jack Davies, who introduced top-quality champagne into the Californian wine repertoire. Beautiful gardens at Chateau Montelena (below and facing page bottom) enchant visitors. Overleaf: vineyards stretching the length of the Napa Valley.

These pages: Clos Pegase Winery, just south of Calistoga in the Napa Valley. Owner Jan Shrem loves art as much as he loves wine, and his office (center left) and the winery's tasting room (bottom left) have the air of an art gallery. Looking midway between a factory and a cathedral, the Clos Pegase winery building (below), commissioned by Shrem and built in 1986, has provoked a great deal of controversy. The building is not designed purely for looks and is highly functional. It sits upon an extensive network of caves, which Jan Shrem uses to age his wines and hang his pictures. On the labels of Clos Pegase wines you will find the house logo, Odilon Redon's Pegasus. The Vichon vineyards (overleaf) sweep dramatically down to the Napa Valley floor. Vichon Winery is best known for Chevrignon, its blend of Sauvignon Blanc and Semillon.

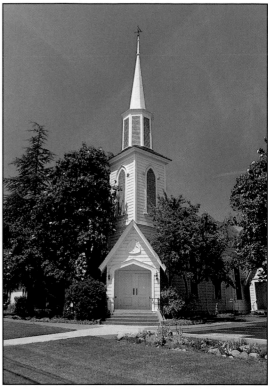

St. Helena (these pages), ringed by the highest density of the valley's vineyards, takes its name from the snow-capped Mt. St. Helena. Robert Louis Stevenson, author of Kidnapped and Treasure Island, spent his honeymoon in St. Helena in 1880. He evidently enjoyed the local wines as he referred to the "vinous bonanzas" of the area. The 1st Presbyterian Church of St. Helena (above) was built in 1860 for $50. Visitors touring the Napa Valley today can overnight at the Ambrose-Bierce Bed and Breakfast (below) en route along the valley. The Italian Ristorante Tra Vigne (facing page), St. Helena, rises above the surrounding vines and doubtless offers many local wines.

Greystone Cellars Winery (facing page and center right) was built in 1888. In 1950 Greystone was bought by The Christian Brothers, a religious teaching order, who produced a wide variety of highly respected wines and "champagnes." The Christian Brothers sold the winery to Heublein Inc. in 1989 for a record $200 million. The splendid Victorian house at Spring Mountain Vineyards (above, below, and bottom right) became internationally famous in the television series Falcon Crest. Chateau Boswell (top right), just north of St. Helena, produces Cabernet Sauvignon and a Chardonnay. Overleaf: vineyards cover 31,000 acres of the Napa Valley.

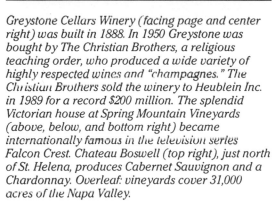

Charles Krug Winery (facing page top), built in 1861, is one of the original Napa Valley estates. V. Sattui had remarkable success with his Napa Valley winery (facing page bottom), started in 1975, by providing a picnic area and selling local breads and cheeses to accompany his wines. Chateau Boswell (below) produces Cabernet Sauvignon and a Chardonnay. Rhine House (overleaf), at the Beringer Winery, was built in 1883 by the German winemakers Frederick and Jacob Beringer as a replica of their ancestral home in Mainz.

Grgich-Hills Cellar (top left), founded in 1977, receives international acclaim for its Chardonnay. Georges Latour founded the Beaulieu Vineyard (center left) in Rutherford in 1900. He brought winemaking expertise from Bordeaux and caused a sensation with his Cabernet Sauvignon. The Rossi Vineyard (bottom left) is another Rutherford property. Mumm Napa Valley (above, below, and facing page) is the highest profile French champagne house to have invested in California. Mumm is one of the most modern champagne producers in the world with its many shining stainless steel fermentation tanks (below) from which its four Napa Valley wines are blended.

The peaceful, monastic exterior of the Robert Mondavi Winery (below) belies its founder's great energy. The winery, founded in 1966, has expanded three times over. Mondavi is a great believer in the importance of aging wine in European oak, rather than Californian woods which have less character. Groth Winery (top right) is one of a cluster of wine producers around Yountville, north of Napa. The small but successful estate, which produces 40,000 cases a year, is run by Dennis Groth, who was formerly chief financial officer for Atari, the computer manufacturer. Far Niente (center right), Italian for "without a care," is a fine old winery built in 1885 in the Oakville/Rutherford area. It is on the National Register of Historic Places and has been meticulously restored by the present owner and wine-maker, Gil Nickel. Auberge du Soleil (bottom right), restaurant and hotel, at Rutherford could not be closer to the heart of the Napa Valley and must be an ideal center from which to tour the area's vineyards. It certainly affords a wonderful view of the valley (overleaf).

S. Anderson Vineyard (facing page top), Yountville, with its beautiful house and rose garden is a family concern, famous for its sparkling wines. Viewing the beautiful and unspoilt Napa Valley from a balloon (below and facing page bottom) is a popular way of seeing its glorious 31,000 acres of vineyards. Domaine Chandon (above, top right, and center right), also in Yountville, is a champagne winery owned by Moët-Hennessy. Antique equipment from France decorates the winery and there is a top-quality French restaurant. Bottom right: Robert Sinskey's Yountville winery, completed in 1988.

Established in 1987, Chimney Rock Winery (above left and bottom left), lying above the Silverado Trail, is a relative newcomer to the area. The Silverado Trail, north of Napa, is a popular vacationers' center. Hotels include the Meadowood Resort (center left) and the Silverado Resort (above). Stag's Leap Wine Cellars (below) produces award-winning Cabernet Sauvignon and Chardonnay. Wide spacing of the vines in the Silverado Trail vineyards (facing page top and overleaf) enables harvesting machines to pass between the rows. The cooler climate of the Carneros region (facing page bottom), southwest of Napa, lends a distinctive flavor to the grapes.

At the beginning of the Californian wine boom in the 1970s, grapes were hardly grown in Santa Barbara County at all. Now, Santa Barbara vineyards (below) stretch over 9,000 acres. Though the San Luis Obispo Valley has a longer history of grape growing than Santa Barbara, they have now emerged as equal partners. The Maison Deutz Winery (top right), south of San Luis Obispo, is a joint American and French company producing one sparkling wine, Brut Cuvée. Bonny Doon Winery (center right) near Santa Cruz is a specialist company mainly producing wines based on those of the Rhone Valley in southeastern France. The Story Winery (bottom right), in Shenandoah Valley, was founded in 1973 by Eugene Story. When tasting wine (overleaf), the nose is just as important as the palate; first, the taster tests the wine for its aroma, i.e., the smell of the grapes, and then for any bouquet, the underlying, more subtle smell which comes from the aging of the wine and from the quality of wood used for the casks and barrels.